# LAZARUS AND
# HIS BELOVED

# LAZARUS AND HIS BELOVED

A ONE-ACT PLAY BY

## KAHLIL GIBRAN

*with
Introduction by the author's
cousin and namesake Kahlil Gibran
and his wife Jean Gibran*

HEINEMANN : LONDON

William Heinemann Ltd
15 Queen Street, Mayfair, London W1X 8BE

LONDON   MELBOURNE   TORONTO
JOHANNESBURG   AUCKLAND

Drawings and photographs from private collection of
Kahlil Gibran, Boston, Mass.
Several excerpts from Minis-Gibran materials in the
Southern Historical Collection, University of North
Carolina, Chapel Hill.

434 29080 7

Printed Offset Litho in Great Britain
by Cox & Wyman Ltd,
London, Fakenham and Reading

# INTRODUCTION

Kahlil Gibran was forty-six years old when *Lazarus and His Beloved*, a one-act play, was read to a private audience. The great events of his life had occurred. The intense dialogue and correspondence with his friends and followers had flowed and showed signs of ebbing. The worldwide hunger for *The Prophet* was beginning to stir. And he knew he was dying. Concern for the terrible adventure is evident in this play where the author openly flirts with, and is ultimately seduced by, death. Through the biblical character Lazarus, Gibran comes to terms with his approaching end — symbolically considers a reprieve (perhaps through the "hygienic" life which his mentor and friend Mary Haskell had always preached, perhaps through medical skill) and then rejects this earth, "this winter."

He speaks through the dead man returned, "There is no dream here and there is no awakening. You and I and this garden are but an illusion, a shadow of the real. The awakening is there, where I was with my beloved and the reality."

Gibran's life — though easily romanticized — had been fractured by the culture shock experienced by all immigrants who floundered to the United States at the end of the nineteenth century. If the bright and impressionable twelve-year-old boy had stayed in Boston public schools and undergone a sustained period of acculturization, his language and style would have been set by competent authorities on American citizenship. But the process of his Americanization was only three years old when Gibran returned alone to Beirut, where he studied at Madrasat Al-Hikmat (School of Wisdom) from 1898 to 1901.

7

During these years of early adolescence, Gibran's vision of his native country and its future was shaped. The tyranny of the Ottoman Empire, the hypocrisy of the organized Church, the subservient role of the Middle Eastern woman created a point of view from which would spring so much of his Arabic writing. Gibran left his native country again when he was nineteen. Despite longings and promises to return, he never did. Aloofness from the local scene—away from Lebanon and speaking to it, removed from Boston and writing to it—was a partial key to his personal expression. This self-removal from society was characteristic of his life and gave him liberty to blend two cultural experiences into one.

Gibran's first of two stays in Paris lasted from 1901 to 1902. There in his twentieth year, the seeds for his first major work, *Spirits Rebellious*, were germinated. This book, eventually written in Boston and published in New York, contained four contemporary parables—thinly disguised attacks on the eroding institutions he had recently witnessed. To the average Westerner, long familiar with the romantic exhortations of revolutionary poets, these words were tame. To the people of a small Middle Eastern province—controlled by dogmatist priests and alien officials of the Turkish Empire—they represented the wildest insubordination. Bold and without precedent, *Spirits Rebellious* was pronounced in Beirut as "dangerous, revolutionary and poisonous to youth." Condemnation and threatened excommunication from the Maronite church were the author's punishment.

This retaliation suddenly identified Gibran as the voice of hope and freedom for oppressed peoples throughout the Middle East. The consequences of excommunication to a young student who had worked in the liberty of Paris and who had known the civil rights of Boston were negligible. His reaction—"an excellent reason for immediately printing a second edition"—was surely the beginning of Gibran's Westernization.

Although he outwardly disregarded his critics, he was inwardly bruised by them. In 1908 he wrote to a cousin living in Brazil:

> The people in Syria are calling me heretic, and the intelligentsia in Egypt vilifies me, saying, "He is the enemy of just laws, of family ties, and of old traditions." Those writers are telling the truth because I do not love man-made laws and I abhor the traditions that our ancestors left us. . . . I know that the principles upon which I base my writings are echoes of the spirit of the great majority of people of the world. . . . Will my teaching ever be received by the Arab world or will it die away and disappear like a shadow?

The formative period in Paris was shattered when Gibran gained from the Turkish consul-general forebodings of the tragedies that would destroy his family. His youngest sister, fifteen-year-old Sultanna, was dead from tuberculosis. Immediately Gibran returned to Boston. His older half-brother Peter, a struggling shopkeeper who had attempted to provide for his sisters and mother, was dying from tuberculosis. His adoring and adored mother, Kamilah Gibran, was fatally ill with a malignant tumor. Only his sister Marianna remained well, and she was traumatized by the disease and poverty the New World was offering her small clan. Between March and June of 1903, Gibran and his sister buried their brother and mother, settled the debts of the meager household, and formed the supportive relationship which was to sustain them until Gibran's death in 1931. In the early years Marianna sponsored his art by sewing for Miss Teahan's Gowns, an elegant Newbury Street establishment. Owing to her efforts, Gibran was able to pursue his early artistic and literary career amid the crowded tenements of Boston's South End.

In the spring of 1904 Gibran assembled a group of drawings, and he was invited by Fred Holland Day, a fashionable photographer, to exhibit them in Day's studio. On the last day of the exhibit Mary Elizabeth Haskell, headmistress of the Marlborough Street Haskell-Dean School for Girls, visited the show and met Gibran. She invited him to transfer his drawings to her school so that her girls would have the opportunity to see the beginning works of a young artist.

This meeting between the twenty-one-year-old creator still clinging to his native language and the thirty-one-year-old schoolmarm—daughter of a Southern gentleman and one educated in the blue-stocking environs of Wellesley College — presaged a long and meaningful relationship. Through Mary Haskell, Gibran was introduced to the American way of life, of thinking, and especially of talking. She was his special tutor, faithful correspondent, and material benefactress. From their letters and from her journal so carefully nurtured from 1904 onward, one can trace Gibran's growth from a provincial Arabic writer, speaking of problems limited to a particular geographic area, to an American writer of commanding English, expressing universal ideals and concerns.

Their letters echo the pride and care with which Mary Haskell encouraged Gibran. In 1911 she wrote, "His English is faulty in pronunciation, and in grammatical number, third person singular and the singular of plural nouns." Their meetings, whether at the Back Bay school or later in his Greenwich Village studio, were marked by her meticulous coaching of his spoken word. Again from Mary's journal: "He read in Nietzche of August, of poets, of scholars . . . Kahlil reads to no one else in English very naturally; for he still makes what for an English-born would be many mis-stresses." When he finally began to write in English, her precise annotations helped him in perfecting each venture.

Fri. Jan. 12, 1917 N.Y.

Beloved Mary

I am sending you another little thing—a parable—to read and correct its English—when you have the time. You see, I go to your school, too, and I am sure that I could not have written a word in English if it were not for you. But I must learn a great deal more before I can give form to my thoughts in this wonderful language. . . . My English is still very limited. But I can learn. I am full of work, Mary, and with God's help and your blessings, I will fulfill the little spark in me.

Love from,<br>Kahlil

11

In 1908 Gibran left for Paris again. This time he was comforted by modest checks forthcoming regularly from Mary Haskell. From 1909 to 1910 he studied at the School of Beaux Arts and the Julian Academy. Gibran met and drew several artists and writers. Among them were Rodin, Debussy, Maeterlinck, Henri de Rochefort. This practice of drawing well-known contemporaries continued throughout his career. Sarah Bernhardt, Albert Ryder, William Butler Yeats, Carl Jung, Ruth St. Denis, John Masefield, Edwin Markham were part of his eminent portfolio.

Upon his return to Boston, Gibran found a studio on West Cedar Street in the Beacon Hill section of the city. His relocation away from the heavily ethnic South End betrayed an attempt to identify himself as an artist, one unencumbered by the clanship where the Lebanese clustered. However, Marianna missed the sidewalk life of her community, the familiar spice-laden stores, her relatives, and her native tongue. Gibran agreed to let her return to her own life and gave up hopes of maintaining a household where he and his sister would live together.

In 1911 Gibran moved to New York City. There he lived for the rest of his life. With the exception of trips to Boston for dutiful visits with his two "Marys" (Marianna and Mary Haskell), and summer vacations shared by his sister and kin, he worked in his studio-apartment at 51 West Tenth Street—a building built for, and eventually owned by, resident painters and writers.

By 1912 *Broken Wings* was published in Arabic. The story of Selma Karami's love for a student and her forced betrothal and marriage to the nephew of an opportunistic bishop often has been interpreted as auto-biographical. Mary Haskell, writing in 1911, quoted Gibran's denial of this.

> Not one of the experiences in the book has been mine. Not one of the characters has been studied from a model, nor one of the events taken from real life.... It is in the first person—no name for the hero.... I thought of this book first about three weeks after you spoke to me of Paris. I made the bare outline of it before I went and in Paris I wrote it. And this summer I rewrote it. And you were always with it—so you see—you are in a way the mother of the little book.

Even with this declaration, fifty years later the precise identification of Selma and the student is of no particular importance. The impact of *Broken Wings* upon the Arab world was and remains great because here for the first time the cloistered Arabic women had the opportunity to identify with a righteous wife who defied the authority of an arranged marriage. The first edition of *Broken Wings* was dedicated to MEH—the mysterious muse of Gibran's creative genesis.

Although Gibran made no attempt to hide MEH (Mary Elizabeth Haskell), her presence in his life was shadowy. As his drawings and paintings multiplied, he often inscribed MEH in their lower right corners. MEH was privy to the most intimate details of his life, from the momentous creations to the trivia of his daily ablutions. They enjoyed each other; openly met in each other's home; visited the museums of Boston and

New York; attended concerts; dined at favorite restaurants. Yet she remained apart from his growing social involvement. Of course, she knew of all the characters in Gibran's life, the Arab-speaking writers, the American admirers; and she wrote thoroughly of them. It is just that the characters did not know of her. And Gibran, unless closely questioned, did not choose to tell. MEH was his special eye and ear, and he selfishly protected their shared privacy.

The next years were productive and full of the dichotomies that marked Gibran's life. Along with his Arabic writing, he continued to perfect his English and to exhibit as an artist. The Great War had deeply affected Lebanon's future. He was the unofficial commentator for the Syrian community in America and was obliged to contribute articles to the Arabic-language magazines and newspapers.

In 1914, Gibran wrote Mary Haskell:

The real truth is this . . . that I am a little chaotic inside. I have a notebook filled with things that came to me those days when I was doing the drawings. . . . They are waiting to be worked on. My *Madman* is on my brain— I want next to have him published—The Syrian question, as you know, is always with me—I'm living this war—The exhibit is on. [His first New York exhibition of paintings and drawings was held at the Montross Gallery, December fourteenth to thirtieth, 1914. Ed.] I have already visions crowding on me of new pictures.

As Gibran matured, his outlook to the East dimmed. Indeed, Pierre Loti, a French novelist enamored with the East, told Gibran, "You are becoming more brutal and less Oriental, and it is bad—too bad."

The brutality that Loti saw was the hardening of the Western Gibran. Time and again Gibran deliberately chose the impenetrable armor of occidental "brutality" when prodding his people to throw off the oppressor's yoke. In his most bitter tirades, Gibran taunted the patience and submission of the oriental mind and challenged his countrymen to action, to retaliation, to revolution. That he had learned to admire the boldness of the West can be inferred from the following lines from his poem *My Countrymen.*

. . .
I have pitied your weakness, My
Countrymen, but my pity has but
Increased your feebleness, exalting
And nourishing slothfulness which
Is vain to Life. And today I see
Your infirmity which my soul loathes
And fears.

. . .
Hypocrisy is your religion, and
Falsehood is your life, and
Nothingness is your ending; why,
Then, are you living? Is not
Death the sole comfort of the
Miserables?

. . .

> Humanity is a brilliant river
> Singing its way and carrying with
> It the mountains' secrets into
> The heart of the sea; but you,
> My Countrymen, are stagnant
> Marshes infested with insects
> And vipers.

. . .

By 1918 he was ready to present his first English work, *The Madman—His Parables and Poems*. The close collaboration between Mary and Gibran on *The Madman* and simultaneously on the "Counsels"—known to posterity as *The Prophet*—permeated their lives.

Gibran still brooded over the fate of his people, who had endured oppression, war, and finally famine. In June 1918 he wrote to MEH, "I have been doing so many things during the past two weeks that I feel rather tired out. There is such a gulf between the Syrian work and my own work. I have to cross that gulf every day and that is the thing that tires me. . . . I might be able to work on my 'Counsels' while resting. . . . I shall send them to you as soon as they take form."

After *The Madman*, Gibran's English books surged: *Twenty Drawings*, 1919; *The Forerunner*, 1920; and finally, in 1923, *The Prophet*—an effort conceived when he was an adolescent, written but unpublished in Arabic when he was a student in Lebanon, and then redeveloped and rewritten in English from 1918 to 1922.

Shortly before *The Prophet* was published, the close relationship between Mary Haskell and Gibran began to waver. Mary, who brilliantly had directed Miss Haskell's School for Girls and then, in Cambridge, the Cambridge-Haskell School, was pressured by her widowed cousin-by-marriage, J. Florance Minis, to give up the Spartan life of a headmistress and become his companion. A wealthy and sophisticated businessman from Savannah, Georgia, Mr. Minis offered Mary a life free from financial and educational responsibilities.

Although the earlier letters and journals of Mary and Kahlil were studded with considerations and frank discussions of their possible marriage, Mary's equivocation over their age difference always had prevailed. Their candidness in considering an intimate affair and their apparent rejection of a sexual relationship had thrust their intimacy on a plane of intellectual friendship. Gibran's pride and his sincere concern for Mary's well-being probably prevented him from influencing her decision to leave Boston. Her departure to the South in 1922 was based on a trial proposal. She lived in Savannah, caring for Florance Minis, and occasionally leaving it to travel with him, for three years before their marriage in 1926.

Mary had relinquished her freedom to visit the New York studio. Yet the letters between her and Kahlil never ceased. Tenderness and respect prevailed, but the easy adoring phrases that had begun the earlier letters—"Dear old elephant-eared partner!" . . . "Dear Old Man!" . . . "Blessed & Beloved Kahlil" . . . "Dearly Beloved Mary"—were to dwindle to "Kahlil" and "Dear Mary."

In one journal entry Mary quoted Gibran's wistful concern about addressing her in future letters: "If one thing has been opened, another may be—and our relationship is so solid and so rich in reality beyond words—that I could call you 'Dear Miss Haskell' and it wouldn't make a bit of difference."

Throughout *The Prophet*'s progress, Mary continued to prune final drafts and galley proofs. Gibran always confirmed Mary's benign influence. Less than a month before his death he wrote her of his soon-to-be-published *The Earth Gods:* "I must turn over the manuscript and the drawings within a month. I wonder if you should care to see the manuscript with your seeing eyes and lay your knowing hands upon it before it is submitted?"

The kinship between MEH and Gibran did not prevent his seeking out other sources for intellectual companionship and strength. In 1920 Gibran founded an association of Arabic writers that was known as *Arrabitah-al-Alimia* (Bond of Writers). Their preamble stated, "This new movement aiming to transport our literature from stagnation to life, from imitation to creation is worthy of all encouragement. It is the hope of Today which shall be the foundation of Tomorrow."

As Gibran's reputation grew, a vigorous social life occupied him in New York. *The Prophet* attracted a special following. Dr. Norman Guthrie, pastor in Manhattan at St. Mark's in the Bowery, was among the first of the American clergy to introduce Gibran's works. After hearing Gibran read from *The Prophet* at St. Mark's, Barbara Young, the proprietor of a bookstore and a former English teacher, entered his life. During Gibran's remaining eight years, she actively participated in his studio. After his death, she became literary executrix of his unpublished writings, traveled to his birthplace in Lebanon, and recorded her impressions of Gibran in *This Man from Lebanon*.

By 1925, Gibran was thoroughly committed to his adopted language. He completed *Sand and Foam* in 1926 and *Jesus The Son of Man* in 1928. As far back as 1914, Gibran had alluded to writing a poem on Lazarus and his "only love." In describing Gibran's ideas for an Arabic version of the poem, MEH recorded the outline of this theme on April 26, 1914: "It is Lazarus of the Bible—and the three days during which he was dead. He went then into his own soul world. There he met the woman he loved and lived with her. But the power of the world-god compelled him back to earth and earth-life." Although a great portion of his writing was based on dialogue, the English version of the one-act play *Lazarus* was Gibran's first attempt to organize his vision in drama form.

The Haskell journals remain mute as to exactly when Gibran converted his earlier Arabic poem "Lazarus" into its final version, an English play. Positive evidence of the play's existence can be traced to a hurried entry that MEH made on May 13, 1926, six days after her marriage to J. Florance Minis. The Minises were staying in New York prior to embarking on an European tour, and Mary wrote, "F. [Florance] to lunch ... while I saw Gibran. G. read me his "Lazarus" [1 act play] . . . Greatly moved in reading Lazarus whose three days of release mirror his own dreams. . . ."

Fortunately for the history of this play, Alma Reed wrote a description of the reading of *Lazarus* at a private celebration of Gibran's forty-sixth birthday. The detailed account appeared in Mrs. Reed's book *Orozco*. Her description of Gibran's friendship with

19

the Mexican painter José Orozco highlights the common ties which the two artists shared. Both Gibran and Orozco—champions of the peasant in their native lands—were living in the urban environment of New York. The studios of both men, Orozco's "Ashram" and Gibran's "Hermitage," were meeting places for contemporary thinkers, revolutionaries, and socialites. Uncomfortable labels had been stamped on their respective geniuses: Orozco was termed "the Mexican Goya" by the critic José Juan Tablada; Gibran, "a new

[William] Blake," according to a statement attributed to Auguste Rodin. Each artist cherished the friendship of a devoted American lady—Orozco, that of Alma Reed; Gibran, that of Mary Haskell.

The birthday recitation of *Lazarus* took place at the Ashram on the evening of January 6, 1929. In her book published in 1956 by the Oxford University Press, Alma Reed described Gibran's appearance: "He spoke fluent French and a colorful English, enriching both languages with the glowing imagery of Arabic

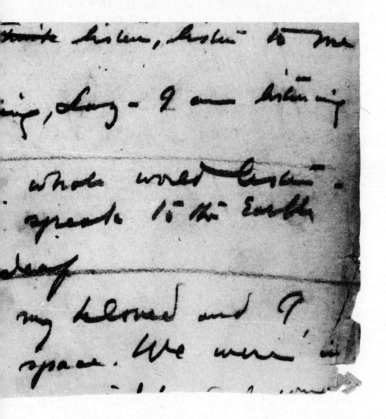

Passage from original manuscript of *Lazarus and His Beloved*.

literature. Slender, brown-eyed, and small-featured, the Lebanese poet with his cosmopolitan manners, European attire, and tiny Parisian mustache was often mistaken for a Frenchman."

That night the "Delphic group," devoted to the exploration of Greek and Oriental philosophies, had come together. Present were Claude Bragdon, Orozco, the Dutch poet Van Noppen, a Hindu disciple of Gandhi — Madame Sarojini Naidu, and several members of the New York Craftsman's Poetry Group. A Mrs. Belle Baker read from *The Prophet* and then "from an unpublished manuscript *Lazarus*" and Gibran's latest book, *Jesus The Son of Man*.

Then Gibran read "The Fox," Orozco's favorite parable from *The Madman*. The events of this congenial evening were intensified by Gibran's faltering in his recitation and suddenly leaving the admiring audience. Orozco and Mrs. Reed found him sobbing in the adjoining room. Gibran confessed to his friends a loss of faith in his creative powers. "I know the truth and I face it. I can no longer write as I once did."

Alma Reed tried to console him, and she comments: "We thought *The Prophet* and the portions of his latest work, *Lazarus*, which Mrs. Baker had just read to us in manuscript, as great as the parables." Then Orozco spoke. "'*Hombre*', he said, as he held the poet in one of those cordial, familiar abrazos . . . 'don't regret that your latest work is different from your early work. I find it good — in fact, wonderful — that you change. It would indeed be a calamity if you did not. Who knows — your new work may be even better than your old. Give it time. You are not the sole judge of its worth. Meanwhile, be happy that you are still

22

young enough to grow — that you are not an ossified academican. To stagnate even at a good point is living death for the artist!'"

And so, Alma Reed reported, the two artists returned to the group, "their faces wreathed in smiles."

This scene of reassurance between Gibran and Orozco is all the more poignant since we learn from Alma Reed that Gibran secretly knew he was mortally sick. "Unknown to us then, [he] had just been advised by his physician that he was in the grip of a serious ailment."

Two days later Gibran was again feted, this time by a gala group at the Hotel McAlpin. The formal photo taken at the lavish dinner shows Gibran elegant

TESTIMONIAL DINNER TENDERED
GIBRAN KAHLIL GIBRAN
ON THE TWENTY-FIFTH YEAR OF HIS
LITERARY AND ARTISTIC ACTIVITIES
HOTEL McALPIN          JANUARY 5, 192

but withdrawn, assured yet restrained. His restraint is reflected in *Lazarus*—especially by the onlooking Madman. The role of the Madman—*majnun* in Arabic; recalling Leila's beloved in the Persian tale *Leila and Majnun*—persists throughout Gibran's work. It is through him that the voice of wisdom often is heard.

Gibran's personal involvement with the mad appears in this letter sent to his colleague Mikhail Naimy:

> So you are on the verge of madness. This is a piece of news magnificent in its fearfulness, fearful in its magnificence and beauty. I say that madness is the first step towards divine sublimation. Be mad, Mischa. Be mad and tell us of the mysteries behind the veil of "reason." Life's purpose is to bring us nearer to those mysteries; and madness is the surest and the quickest steed. Be mad, and remain a mad brother to your mad brother.

In *Lazarus*, the Madman, unlike his predecessor in *John the Madman*, does not insert himself into the action. He is a commentator—without involvement or pity. Not even motherly love or sisterly anguish can pull him into the ordinary scheme of things.

Gibran once said to MEH, "A tremendous number of names significant in my life begin with "M". It was the root letter of a root name in my mother's family; . . . the steamer line we sailed on—and the steamer; my two best teachers; my sister Mary's name; your name; Marthe M. [the young widow whose spirit was with him so much in his youth]; Micheline [Mary Haskell's young teacher of whom Gibran was so fond. ED.]; the Mortens, etc., etc."

In retrospect one recalls the names, too, of both May Ziadeh, the Egyptian journalist with whom Gibran corresponded, and Mikhail Naimy, the beloved "Mischa" poet and biographer of Gibran. And in this late one-act play itself, two more M's appear: Martha, simple and industrious in her love for her brother; Mary, probing and conversant with his anguish.

Throughout his writings, Gibran had regularly offered paeans of thanksgiving to Motherhood—"The most beautiful word on the lips of mankind is the word 'Mother'. . . . The mother is everything. . . . She is the source of love, mercy, sympathy, and forgiveness."

In *Lazarus* even this earthly enthusiasm is discarded. The terseness of language between the devoted mother and her miraculously returned son shows the estrangement in his heart. Most important is his rejection of her pleas to eat the prepared lentils—a final denial of life. In Gibran's play, Lazarus, then, is not just a man miraculously restored to life. He symbolizes a search for more; an attempted reconciliation with a beloved spirit; a reunification with, not the Godhead, but a specific someone—in the firmament.

After the 1929 reading, *Lazarus* remained unseen for decades. Gibran worked fervently during his remaining two years. His commitment to the West and to his continued expression in English was confirmed as he wrote to MEH in November 1929: "My responsibilities in the East are over. And I assure you Mary that I shall not undertake anything of that sort unless I am absolutely certain of my tomorrow. It was in my heart to help a little because I was helped much."

Gibran completed *The Earth Gods* in 1931. His final version of *The Wanderer*, in Mary's hands at his death, was published posthumously in 1932. *The Garden of the Prophet* appeared that same year. On April 10, 1931, at 11:00 p.m., Gibran died. Although debilitated by cirrhosis of the liver and incipient tuberculosis, he had rejected hospitalization until the last day. On that morning he was finally brought to St. Vincent's Hospital in Greenwich Village. All that Barbara Young, Mischa Naimy, his sister Marianna, and his Boston cousins Rose Diab and Assaf George could do was to wait. The next day Marianna telegraphed MEH, living in Savannah, about the poet's death. Despite reservations on the part of her husband, Mary Haskell Minis rejoined Gibran and the studio on Monday, April 13.

The following events—the train journey from New York to Boston; the funeral services at the South End Maronite church, Our Lady of the Cedars; the temporary internment in Forest Hills Cemetery; the cortege to Providence, Rhode Island, from which Marianna and her cousins launched the long pilgrimage by sea to Beirut; and finally the triumphant procession from Beirut to Besharri, where Gibran was buried at last on August 21 at Mar Sarkis, a Carmelite monastery where he once had worshipped—all have often been recounted.

After the Boston funeral service, MEH, Marianna, and her cousin Rose Diab returned to New York. There with Barbara Young, the details of Gibran's studio, his estate, and will were examined. Gibran's last will, dated March 10, 1930, a will now famous for its largesse to the author's birthplace, reflected his philosophy "It was in my heart to help a little because I was helped much."

To Marianna:

I wish that whatever money or securities Mr. Edgar Speyer has been gracious enough to hold for me should go to my sister Mary K. Gibran who now lives at 76 Tyler Street, Boston, Mass.

There are also 40 (forty) shares of the Fifty-One West Tenth Street Studio Association stock lying in my safe deposit box with the Bank of Manhattan Trust Company, 31 Union Square, New York. These shares are also going to my sister.

To Besharri:

There are in addition to the foregoing 2 (two) bank books of the West Side Savings Bank, 422 Sixth Avenue, New York which I have with me in my studio. I wish that my sister would take this money to my home town of Besharri, Republic of Lebanon, and spend it upon charities.

The royalties on my copyrights, which copyrights I understand can be extended upon request by my heirs for an additional period of twenty-eight years after my death, are to go to my home town.

To Mary Haskell:

Everything found in my studio after my death, pictures, books, objects of art, et cetera, go to Mrs. Mary Haskell Minis, now living at 24 Gaston Street West, Savannah, Ga. But I would like to have Mrs. Minis send all or any part of those things to my home town should she see fit to do so.

Mary Haskell's and Barbara Young's simultaneous discovery of the letters from MEH to Gibran created a crisis of personality. Shocked by their existence, Barbara asked that this evidence of their mutual confidences be burned. Mary Haskell assented. Then realizing its historical and literary implications, she returned to the studio hours before her trip to Savannah and rescued the testament of their years together.

Mary Haskell's concern for, and generosity toward, Gibran's posterity and Marianna's future were evidenced by her gift to Marianna of the many brown notebooks in which Gibran had written. To Marianna she wrote: "I am sending you the little brown notebooks found in the corner of the studio. . . ."

Though Marianna was grateful, she personally could not respond. Like Martha with her loom, she had cared for her brother with her hands—stitching so that Kahlil could write down his stories.

Marianna, who had listened to him read, who had heard great men praise her brother's literary contributions, was never herself to read his words. She simply had never learned to read Arabic or English.

Her brother's manuscripts, his letters to her, the drawings that she owned, were carefully put away in cardboard boxes—for another Gibran to discover.

The cruel fact of Marianna's helplessness in literary matters made communications for Mary Haskell most difficult. As her letters to Marianna diminish, Mary's frustration over the ironic silence seems implicit. Both Marys lived long lives. Mary Haskell died at the age of ninety-one in a Georgia nursing home in 1964. Marianna lived to be eighty-seven, and died in a Boston nursing home in 1972.

Marianna's world centered around her relatives: the Boston cousins Maroon and Assaf George, Zakieh Gibran (known as Rose Diab), Nicholas Gibran, and Rose Gibran. Never having married, she regarded as her own the children of her cousins Nicholas and Rose.

Nicholas Gibran (identified in Barbara Young's *This Man from Lebanon* as the creator of a desk in Gibran's native church—"There is a reading desk that was carved by my cousin N'Oula, the same N'Oula who is the father of my godchild, the little Kahlil") and Rose Gibran were second cousins. Their marriage, in Boston, produced five children all named by the poet — Horace, Susanne, Kahlil, Selma, and Hafiz. Nicholas supported the family as a carpenter, and Rose contributed by working in a garment factory near their South End apartment.

The precarious years of the Depression were alleviated by the endless stories about their famous relative. "Aunt Marianna" lightened Rose's burden by caring for the boys during summer vacations. Annually she treated each boy to a visit in the country so he could escape the slum streets. Gibran's godchild Kahlil was carefully watched and encouraged.

This middle son — the author's namesake — grew up in a world filled with the objects and legends of Gibran's Boston days. He learned from his father the art of tools and from "Aunt Marianna" the life of the poet. Slowly she began to entrust this Kahlil with the letters and stories she could not read, and with the paintings and drawings he loved so much.

As Gibran's godson grew, his personal career as a sculptor took shape. His concerns were with his own studio, and with his own development as an artist. Yet the gifts of the brown books and the typed manuscripts were forever present and pressed his conscience.. He knew that he must someday present them to the world in the spirit of honesty and dignity with which they were given.

Thus, this publication of *Lazarus and His Beloved*, one of Kahlil Gibran's last works, introduces a wealth of material which has lain unseen and unknown by the world at large for forty years.

# LAZARUS AND
# HIS BELOVED

"Said I not unto thee that, if thou wouldest believe, thou shouldest see the glory of God?" Then they took away the stone from the place where the dead was laid. And Jesus lifted up his eyes, and said, "Father, I thank thee that thou hast heard me. And I knew that thou hearest me always: but because of the people which stand by I said it, that they may believe that thou hast sent me." And when he thus had spoken, he cried with a loud voice, "Lazarus, come forth!" And he that was dead came forth, bound hand and foot with graveclothes and his face was bound about with a napkin. Jesus saith unto them, "Loose him, and let him go!"

John 9:40–44

# LAZARUS AND HIS BELOVED

*Cast of Characters*

LAZARUS
MARY, HIS SISTER
MARTHA, HIS SISTER
THE MOTHER OF LAZARUS
PHILIP, A DISCIPLE
THE MADMAN

SCENE: The garden outside of the home of Lazarus
and his mother and sisters in Bethany

TIME: Late afternoon of Monday, the day after
the resurrection of Jesus of Nazareth from
the grave

*At curtain rise:* Mary *is at right gazing up toward the hills.*
Martha *is seated at her loom near the house door, left.*
The Madman *is seated around the corner of the house,*
*and against its wall, down left.*

Mary   (*turning to Martha*) You do not work. You have
       not worked much lately.

Martha   You are not thinking of my work. My idleness
         makes you think of what our Master said. Oh, be-
         loved Master!

The       The day shall come when there will be no weaver,
Madman    and no one to wear the cloth. We shall all stand
          naked in the sun.
          (*There is a long silence. The women do not ap-*
          *pear to have heard The Madman speaking. They*
          *never hear him.*)

Mary   It is getting late.

Martha   Yes, yes, I know. It is getting late.
         (*The mother enters, coming out from the house*
         *door.*)

Mother   Has he not returned yet?

Martha   No, mother, he has not returned yet.
         (*The three women look toward the hills.*)

The       He himself will never return. All that you may see
Madman    is a breath struggling in a body.

38

*Mary*   It seems to me that he has not yet returned from the other world.

*Mother*   The death of our Master has affected him deeply, and during these last days he has hardly eaten a morsel, and I know at night that he does not sleep. Surely it must have been the death of our Friend.

*Martha*   No, mother. There is something else; something I do not understand.

*Mary*   Yes, yes. There is something else. I know it, too. I have known it all these days, yet I cannot explain it. His eyes are deeper. He gazes at me as though he were seeing someone else through me. He is tender but his tenderness is for someone not here. And he is silent, silent as if the seal of death is yet upon his lips.

*( A silence falls over the three women. )*

*The Madman*   Everyone looks through everyone to see someone else.

*Mother*   *( breaking the silence )* Would that he'd return. Of late he has spent too many hours among those hills alone. He should be here with us.

*Mary*   Mother, he has not been with us for a long time.

*Martha*   Why, he has always been with us, only those three days!

40

*Mary*  Three days? *Three days!* Yes, Martha, you are right. It was only three days.

*Mother*  I wish my son would return from the hills.

*Martha*  He will come soon, mother. You must not worry.

*Mary*  (*in a strange voice*) Sometimes I feel that he will never come back from the hills.

*Mother*  If he came back from the grave, then surely he will come back from the hills. And oh, my daughters, to think that the One who gave us back his life was slain but yesterday.

*Mary*  Oh, the mystery of it, and the pain of it.

*Mother*  Oh, to think that they could be so cruel to the One who gave my son back to my heart.

(*a silence*)

*Martha*  But Lazarus should not stay so long among the hills:

*Mary*  It is easy for one in a dream to lose his way among the olive groves. And I know a place where Lazarus loved to sit and dream and be still. Oh, mother, it is beside a little stream. If you do not know the place you could not find it. He took me there once, and we sat on two stones, like children. It was spring, and little flowers were growing beside us. We often spoke of that place during the winter

41

season. And each time that he spoke of that place a strange light came into his eyes.

The Madman  Yes, that strange light, that shadow cast by the other light.

Mary  And mother, you know that Lazarus has always been away from us, though he was always with us.

Mother  You say so many things I cannot understand. (*pause*) I wish my son would come back from the hills. I wish he would come back! (*pause*) I must go in now. The lentils must not be overcooked.

(*The mother exits through the house door.*)

Martha  I wish I could understand all that you say, Mary. When you speak it is as though someone else is speaking.

Mary  (*her voice a little strange*) I know, my sister, I know. Whenever we speak it is someone else who is speaking.

(*There is a prolonged silence. Mary is faraway in her thoughts, and Martha watches her half-curiously. Lazarus enters, coming from the hills, back left. He throws himself upon the grass under the almond trees near the house.*)

Mary  (*running toward him*) Oh, Lazarus, you are tired

and weary. You should not have walked so far.

**Lazarus** (*speaking absently*) Walking, walking and going nowhere; seeking and finding nothing. But it is better to be among the hills.

**The Madman** Well, after all it is a cubit nearer to the other hills.

**Martha** (*after a brief silence*) But you are not well, and you leave us all day long, and we are much concerned. When you came back, Lazarus, you made us happy. But in leaving us alone here you turn our happiness into anxiety.

**Lazarus** (*turning his face toward the hills*) Did I leave you long this day? Strange that you should call a moment among the hills a separation. Did I truly stay more than a moment among the hills?

**Martha** You have been gone all day.

**Lazarus** To think, to think! A whole day among the hills! Who would believe it?

(*A silence. The mother enters, coming out from the house door.*)

**Mother** Oh, my son, I am glad you have come back. It is late and the mist is gathering upon the hills. I feared for you, my son.

**The Madman** They are afraid of the mist. And the mist is their beginning and the mist is their end.

43

*Lazarus*    Yes, I have come back to you from the hills. The pity of it, the pity of it all.

*Mother*    What is it, Lazarus? What is the pity of it all?

*Lazarus*    Nothing, mother. Nothing.

*Mother*    You speak strangely. I do not understand you, Lazarus. You have said little since your home-coming. But whatever you have said has been strange to me.

*Martha*    Yes, strange.

*(There is a pause.)*

*Mother*    And now the mist is gathering here. Let us go into the house. Come, my children.

*(The mother, after kissing Lazarus with wistful tenderness, enters the house.)*

*Martha*    Yes, there is a chill in the air. I must take my loom and my linen indoors.

*Mary*    *(sitting down beside Lazarus on the grass under the almond trees, and speaking to Martha)* It is true the April evenings are not good for either your loom or your linen. Would you want me to help you take your loom indoors?

*Martha*    No, no. I can do it alone. I have always done it alone.

44

*(Martha carries her loom into the house, then she returns for the linen, taking that in also. A wind passes by, shaking the almond trees, and a drift of petals falls over Mary and Lazarus.)*

*Lazarus*   Even spring would comfort us, and even the trees would weep for us. All there is on earth, if all there is on earth could know our downfall and our grief, would pity us and weep for us.

*Mary*   But spring is with us, and though veiled with the veil of sorrow, yet *it is* spring. Let us not speak of pity. Let us rather accept both our spring and our sorrow with gratitude. And let us wonder in sweet silence at Him who gave you life yet yielded His own life. Let us not speak of pity, Lazarus.

*Lazarus*   Pity, pity that I should be torn away from a thousand thousand years of heart's desire, a thousand thousand years of heart's hunger. Pity that after a thousand thousand springs I am turned again to this winter.

*Mary*   *What do you mean*, my brother? Why do you speak of a thousand thousand springs? You were but three days away from us. Three short days. But our sorrow was indeed longer than three days.

*Lazarus*   Three days? Three centuries, three aeons! All of

45

time! All of time with the one my soul loved before time began.

| | |
|---|---|
| The Madman | Yes, three days, three centuries, three aeons. Strange they would always weigh and measure. It is always a sundial and a pair of scales. |
| Mary | *(in amazement)* The one your soul loved before time began? Lazarus, why do you say these things? It is but a dream you dreamed in another garden. Now we are here in this garden, a stone's throw from Jerusalem. We are here. And you know well, my brother, that our Master would have you be with us in this awakening to dream of life and love; and He would have you an ardent disciple, a living witness of His glory. |
| Lazarus | There is no dream here and there is no awakening. You and I and this garden are but an illusion, a shadow of the real. The awakening is there where I was with my beloved and the reality. |
| Mary | *(rising)* Your beloved? |
| Lazarus | *(also rising)* My beloved. |
| The Madman | Yes, yes. His beloved, the space virgin, the beloved of everyman. |
| Mary | But where is your beloved? Who is your beloved? |
| Lazarus | My twin heart whom I sought here and did not find. Then death, the angel with winged feet, |

46

came and led my longing to her longing, and I lived with her in the very heart of God. And I became nearer to her and she to me, and we were one. We were a sphere that shines in the sun; and we were a song among the stars. All this, Mary, all this and more, till a voice, a voice from the depths, the voice of a world called me; and that which was inseparable was torn asunder. And the thousand thousand years with my beloved in space could not guard me from the power of that voice which called me back.

*Mary*    (*looking unto the sky*) O blessed angels of our silent hours, make me to understand this thing! I would not be an alien in this new land discovered by death. Say more, my brother, go on. I believe in my heart I can follow you.

*The*    Follow him, if you can, little woman. Shall the
*Madman*    turtle follow the stag?

*Lazarus*    I was a stream and I sought the sea where my beloved dwells, and when I reached the sea I was brought to the hills to run again among the rocks. I was a song imprisoned in silence, longing for the heart of my beloved, and when the winds of heaven released me and uttered me in that green forest I was recaptured by a voice, and I was

48

turned again into silence. I was a root in the dark earth, and I became a flower and then a fragrance in space rising to enfold my beloved, and I was caught and gathered by a hand, and I was made a root again, a root in the dark earth.

*The Madman*  If you are a root you can always escape the tempests in the branches. And it is good to be a running stream even after you have reached the sea. Of course it is good for water to run upward.

*Mary*  *(to herself)* Oh strange, passing strange! *(to Lazarus)* But my brother it is good to be a running stream, and it is good to be a song not yet sung, and it is good to be a root in the dark earth. The Master knew all this and He called you back to us that we may know there is no veil between life and death. Do you not see that you are a living testimony to deathlessness? Can you not see how one word uttered in love may bring together elements scattered by an illusion called death? Believe and have faith, for only in faith, which is our deeper knowledge, can you find comfort.

*Lazarus*  Comfort! Comfort the treacherous, the deadly! Comfort that cheats our senses and makes us slaves to the passing hour! I would not have comfort. I would have passion! I would burn in the cool

49

space with my beloved. I would be in the bound-
less space with my mate, my other self. O Mary,
Mary, you were once my sister, and we knew one
another even when our nearest kin knew us not.
Now listen to me, listen to me with your heart.

Mary     I am listening, Lazarus.

The     Let the whole world listen. The sky will now
Madman     speak to the earth, but the earth is deaf. The earth
is almost as deaf as you and I.

Lazarus     We were in space, my beloved and I, and we were

all space. We were in light and we were all light. And we roamed even like the ancient spirit that moved upon the face of the waters; and it was forever the first day. We were love itself that dwells in the heart of the white silence. Then a voice like thunder, a voice like countless spears piercing the ether, cried out saying, "Lazarus, come forth!" And the voice echoed and re-echoed in space, and I, even as a flood tide became an ebbing tide; a house divided, a garment rent, a youth unspent,

a tower that fell down, and out of its broken stones a landmark was made. A voice cried "Lazarus, come forth!" and I descended from the mansion of the sky to a tomb within a tomb, this body in a sealed cave.

*The*
*Madman*   Master of the caravan, where are your camels and where are your men? Was it the hungry earth that swallowed them? Was it the simoon that shrouded them with sand? No! Jesus of Nazareth raised His hand, Jesus of Nazareth uttered a word; and tell me now, where are your camels and where are your men, and where are your treasures? In the trackless sand, in the trackless sand. But the simoon will come again and unbury them. The simoon will always come again.

*Mary*   Oh, it is like a dream dreamt upon a mountaintop. I know, my brother, I know the world you have visited, though I have never seen it. Yet all that you say is passing strange. It is a tale told by someone across a valley, and I can hardly hear it.

*Lazarus*   It is all so different across the valley. There is no weight there and there is no measure. You are with your beloved.
*(a silence)*
O my beloved! O my beloved fragrance in space!

52

Wings that were spread for me! Tell me, tell me
in the stillness of my heart, do you seek me, and
was it pain to you to be separated from me? Was
I also a fragrance and wings spread in space? And
tell me now, my beloved, was there a double
cruelty, was there a brother of His in another
world who called you from life to death, and had
you a mother and sisters and friends who deemed
it a miracle? Was there a double cruelty performed
in blessedness?

*Mary*   No, no, my brother. There is only one Jesus of
one world. All else is but a dream, even as your
beloved.

*Lazarus*   *(with great passion)* No, no! If He is not a dream
then He is nothing. If He had not known what is
beyond this Jerusalem, then He is nothing. If He
did not know my beloved in space then He was
not the Master. O my friend Jesus, you once gave
me a cup of wine across the table, and you said,
"Drink this in remembrance of me." And you
dipped a morsel of bread in the oil, and you said,
"Eat this, it is of my share of the loaf." O my
friend, you have put your arm on my shoulder and
called me "son." My mother and my sisters have
said in their hearts, "He loves our Lazarus." *And*

*I loved you*. And then you went away to build more towers in the sky, and I went to my beloved. Tell me now, tell me, why did you bring me back? Did you not know in your knowing heart that I was with my beloved? Did you not meet her in your wandering above the summits of Lebanon? Surely you saw her image in my eyes when I came and stood before you at the door of the tomb. And have you not a beloved in the sun? And would you have a greater one than yourself separate you from her? And after separation what would you say? What shall I say to you now?

*The Madman*   He bade me also to come back but I did not obey, and now they call me mad.

*Mary*   Lazarus, Have *I* a beloved in the sky? Has my longing created a being beyond this world? And must I die to be with him? Oh, my brother, tell me, have I a mate also? If this thing be so, how good it is to live and die, and live and die again; if a beloved awaits me, to fulfill all that I am, and I to fulfill all that he is!

*The Madman*   Everywoman has a beloved in the sky. The heart of everywoman creates a being in space.

*Mary*   (*repeating softly as if to herself*) Have I a beloved in the sky?

| | |
|---|---|
| *Lazarus* | I do not know. But if you had a beloved, an other self, somewhere, somewhen, and you should meet him, surely there would not be one to separate you from him. |
| *The Madman* | He may be here, and He may call her. But like many others she may not hear. |
| *Lazarus* | *(coming to center of stage)* To wait, to wait for each season to overcome another season; and then to wait for that season to be overcome by another; to watch all things ending before your own end comes—your end which is your beginning. To listen to all voices, and to know that they melt to silence, all save the voice of your heart that would cry even in sleep. |
| *The Madman* | The children of God married the children of men. Then they were divorced. Now, the children of men long for the children of God. I pity them all, the children of men and the children of God. |

*(a silence)*

| | |
|---|---|
| *Martha* | *(appearing in the doorway)* Why don't you come into the house, Lazarus? Our mother has prepared the supper. *(with a little impatience)* Whenever you and Mary are together you talk and talk and talk, and no one knows what you say. |

*(Martha stands a few seconds, then goes into the house.)*

Lazarus    *(speaking to himself, and as though he has not heard Martha)* Oh, I am spent. I am wasted, I am hungry and I am thirsty. Would that you could give me some bread and some wine.

Mary    *(going to him and putting her arm around him)* I will, I will, my brother. But come into the house. Our mother has prepared the evening meal.

The Madman    He asks for bread which they cannot bake, and wine for which they have no bottles.

Lazarus    Did I say I was hungry and thirsty? I am not hungry for your bread, nor thirsty for your wine. I tell you I shall not enter a house until my beloved's hand is upon the latch of the door. I shall not sit at the feast till *she* be at my side.

*(Mother peers from the house door.)*

Mother    Now, Lazarus, why do you stay out in the mist? And you, Mary, why do you not come into the house? I have lit the candles and the food is upon the board, and yet you will stay out babbling and chewing your words in the dark.

Lazarus    My own mother would have me enter a tomb. She would have me eat and drink and she would even

56

bid me sit among shrouded faces and receive eternity from withered hands and draw life from clay cups.

*The Madman* White bird that flew southward where the sun loves all things, what held you in mid-air, and who brought you back? It was your friend, Jesus of Nazareth. He brought you back out of pity for the wingless who would not be along. Oh, white bird, it is cold here, and you shiver, and the North wind laughs in your feathers.

*Lazarus* You would be in a house and under a roof. You would be within four walls, with a door and a window. You would be here, and you are without vision. Your mind is here, and my spirit is there. All of you is upon the earth; all of me is in space. You creep into houses, and I flew beyond upon the mountaintop. You are all slaves, the one to the other, and you worship but yourselves. You sleep and you dream not; you wake but you walk not among the hills. And yesterday I was weary of you and of your lives, and I sought the other world which you call death, and if I had died it was out of longing. Now, I stand here at this moment, rebelling against that which you call life.

*Martha* (*who has come out of the house while Lazarus was*

57

*speaking*) But the Master saw our sorrow and our pain, and He called you back to us, and yet you rebel. Oh, what cloth, rebelling against its own weaver! What a house rebelling against its own builder!

*Mary*　He knew our hearts and He was gracious unto us, and when He met our mother and saw in her eyes a dead son, buried, then her sorrow held Him, and for a moment He was still, and He was silent. (*pause*) Then we followed Him to your tomb.

*Lazarus*　Yes, it was my mother's sorrow, and your sorrow. It was pity, self-pity, that brought me back. How selfish is self-pity, and how deep: I say that I rebel. I say that divinity itself should not turn spring to winter. I had climbed the hills in longing, and your sorrow brought me back to this valley. You wanted a son and a brother to be with you through life. Your neighbors wanted a miracle. You and your neighbors, like your fathers and your forefathers, would have a miracle, that you may believe in the simplest things in life. How cruel you are and how hard are your hearts, and how dark is the night of your eyes. For *that* you bring down the prophets from their glory to your joys, and then you kill the prophets.

*Martha*  (*with reproof*) You call our sorrow self-pity. What is your wailing but self-pity? Be quiet, and accept the life the Master has given you.

*Lazarus*  He did not give me life, He gave you my life. He took my life from my beloved, and gave it to you, a miracle to open your eyes and your ears. He sacrificed me even as He sacrificed Himself. (*speaking unto the sky*) Father, forgive them. They know not what they do.

*Mary*  (*in awe*) It was He who said those very words, hanging upon the cross.

*Lazarus*  Yes, He said these words for me as for Himself, and for all the unknown who understand and are not understood. Did He not say these words when your tears begged Him for my life? It was your desire and not His will that bade His spirit to stand at the sealed door and urge eternity to yield me unto you. It was that ancient longing for a son and a brother that brought me back.

*Mother*  (*approaches him and puts her arm around his shoulders*) Lazarus, you were ever an obedient son and a loving son. What has happened to you? Be with us, and forget all that troubles you.

*Lazarus*  (*raising his hand*) My mother and my brothers and my sisters are those who hear my words.

| | |
|---|---|
| *Mary* | These are also His words. |
| *Lazarus* | Yes, and He said these words for me as well as for Himself, and for all those who have earth for mother, and sky for father, and for all those who are born free of a people and country and race. |
| *The Madman* | Captain of my ship, the wind filled your sails, and you dared the sea; and you sought the blessed isles. What other wind changed your course, and why did you return to these shores? It was Jesus of Nazareth who commanded the wind with a breath of His own breath, and then filled the sail where it was empty, and emptied it where it was full. |
| *Lazarus* | *(Suddenly he forgets them all, and he raises his head, and opens his arms.)* O my beloved! There was dawn in your eyes, and in that dawn there was the silent mystery of a deep night, and the silent promise of a full day, and I was fulfilled, and I was whole. O my beloved, this life, this veil, is between us now. Must I live this death and die again that I may live again? Must I needs linger until all these green things turn yellow and then naked again, and yet again? *(pause)* Oh, I cannot curse Him. But why, of all men, why should I return? Why should I of all shepherds be driven back into the desert after the green pasture? |

*The*
*Madman*
*Lazarus*

If you were one of those who would curse, you would not have died so young.

Jesus of Nazareth, tell me now, why did you do this to me? Was it fair that I should be laid down, a humble lowly sorrowful stone leading to the height of your glory? Any one of the dead might have served to glorify you. Why have you separated this lover from his beloved? Why did you call me to a world which you knew in your heart you would leave? *(then crying with a great voice)* Why—*why*—*why* did you call me from the living heart of eternity to this living death? O Jesus of Nazareth—I cannot curse you! I cannot curse you. I would bless you.

*(Silence. Lazarus becomes as one whose strength has gone out in a stream. His head falls forward almost upon his breast. After a moment of awe-full silence, he raises his head again, and with a transfigured face he cries in a deep and thrilling voice.)*

Jesus of Nazareth! My friend! We have both been crucified. Forgive me! Forgive me. I bless you—now, and forevermore.

*(At this moment the disciple appears running from the direction of the hills.)*

*Mary*    Philip!

*Philip*    He is risen! The Master is risen from the dead and now He is gone into Galilee.

*The*    He is risen, but He will be crucified again a thou-
*Madman*    sand times.

*Mary*    Philip, my friend, what do you say?

*Martha*    *(rushes toward the disciple, and grasps him by the arms)* How glad I am to see you again. But who has risen? Of whom are you speaking?

*Mother*    *(walking toward him)* Come in, my son. You shall have supper with us this night.

*Philip*    *(unmoved by any of their words)* I say the Master has risen from the dead and has gone into Galilee.

*(A deep silence falls.)*

*Lazarus*    Now you shall *all* listen to me. If He has risen from the dead they will crucify Him again, but they shall not crucify Him alone. Now I shall proclaim Him, and they shall crucify me also.

*(He turns in exaltation and walks in the direction of the hills.)*

My mother and my sisters, I shall follow Him who gave me life until He gives me death. Yes, I too

would be crucified, and that crucifixion will end this crucifixion.

*(a silence)*

Now I shall seek His spirit, and I shall be released. And though they bind me in iron chains I shall not be bound. And though a thousand mothers and a thousand thousand sisters shall hold my garments I shall not be held. I shall go with the East wind where the East wind goes. And I shall seek my beloved in the sunset where all our days find peace. And I shall seek my beloved in the night where all the mornings sleep. And I shall be the one man among all men who twice suffered life, and twice death, and twice knew eternity.

*(Lazarus looks into the face of his mother, then into the faces of his sisters, then at Philip's face; then again at his mother's face. Then as if he were a sleepwalker he turns and runs toward the hills. He disappears. They are all dazed and shaken.)*

*Mother*   My son, my son, come back to me!

*Mary*   My brother, where are you going? Oh come, my brother, come back to us.

*Martha*   *(as if to herself)* It is so dark I know he will lose his way.

63

Mother    *(almost screaming)* Lazarus, my son!

          *(a silence)*

Philip    He has gone where we shall all go. And he shall not return.

Mother    *(going to the very back of the stage, close to where he has disappeared)* Lazarus, Lazarus, my son! *Come back to me! (She shrieks.)*

          *(There is a silence. The running steps of Lazarus are lost in the distance.)*

The
Madman    Now he is gone, and he is beyond your reach. And now your sorrow must seek another. *(He pauses.)* Poor, poor Lazarus, the first of the martyrs, and the greatest of them all.